# THE STORY OF THE FIRST EASTER

THOMAS NELSON PUBLISHERS
Nashville

First published in 1994 by
Thomas Nelson Publishers, Nashville, Tennessee.

**Story retold by Bill Yenne**

Art and design direction by Bill Yenne. Illustrated by Mark
Busacca, Edwin Esquivel, Emi Fukawa, Victor Lee, Doug
Scott, Vadim Vahrameev, Hanako Wakiyama, and Bill Yenne.
Special thanks to Ruth DeJauregui.

Produced by
Bluewood Books (A Division of The Siyeh Group, Inc.)
P.O. Box 460313, San Francisco, CA 94146

Yenne, Bill, 1949-
    The Story of the First Easter/[story retold for this edition
by Bill Yenne].
        p.    cm.—(Children's Bible Classics)
    ISBN 0-7852-8328-5 (MM)—ISBN 0-7852-8332-3 (TR)
    1. Jesus Christ—Resurrection—Juvenile literature.
    2. Jesus Christ—Crucifixion—Juvenile literature.
    3. Bible stories, English—N.T. Gospels.    [1. Jesus
Christ—Resurrection.    2. Jesus Christ—Passion.
    3. Bible stories—N.T.    4. Easter.]    I. Title.    II. Series
BT481.Y45 1994
232.9′7—dc20                                                93-37475
                                                                    CIP
                                                                    AC

97  98—        3  4  5

Printed and bound in the United States of America

# THE STORY OF THE FIRST EASTER

Jesus had been staying in Bethany, where His friends Martha, Mary and Lazarus lived. But He knew that the time had come for Him to go to Jerusalem.

The people in Jerusalem wanted Him to be their king, but Jesus knew that His Father in heaven had something even more important for Him to do.

As Jesus approached Jerusalem, many people went out to meet Him, waving palm branches. The people knew who He was and they were very excited to see Him.

"Hosanna to the son of David!" they shouted. "Blessed is He who comes in the name of the Lord!"

Several days later was Passover. This was the celebration of the holy day when God delivered the children of Israel from the Egyptians. Jesus and His twelve disciples got together at a friend's house in Jerusalem for a special Passover supper.

As they were eating, Jesus took some bread, and He blessed it and broke it. He passed it out to His disciples and He said, "Take this and eat it. This is My body."

Then He took His cup, gave thanks, and said, "All of you drink from it. This is My blood of the covenant, poured out for the forgiveness of sins."

Everybody was happy that they could be together for this special supper, but Jesus seemed sad. He looked around the table at His disciples and said, "One of you will turn Me over to our enemies."

Eleven of His disciples couldn't believe their ears, but Judas knew what Jesus was talking about.

After supper, Jesus took His disciples to the Mount of Olives. Then Peter, James and John went with Jesus to a grove of olive trees called the Garden of Gethsemane. Jesus often went to this place with His disciples to pray and rest.

Jesus went among the trees and knelt down to pray. He asked God the Father to help Him face what He knew was going to happen soon.

When Jesus came back to the three disciples, He found them sleeping and asked them to pray with Him. But they fell asleep again. He went and prayed two more times.

When the disciples awoke, they heard the noise of a crowd and saw the flashing of torches. The crowd was armed with swords, clubs, and spears. Judas rushed out from the crowd and greeted Jesus with a kiss as though he was glad to see Him. The crowd knew Judas would kiss Jesus to betray Him. They grabbed Jesus and arrested Him.

One of the disciples near Jesus drew his sword and cut off the ear of the slave of the high priest. But Jesus said, "No more of this," and healed the slave's ear.

When Jesus' disciples saw that He would not allow them to fight, they ran away. The crowd took Jesus to Caiaphas, the High Priest.

After a mock trial before Caiaphas, the crowd took Jesus to the Roman Governor, Pontius Pilate, who ruled over Judea. He listened to their complaints about Jesus and offered either to set a criminal named Barabbas free or to set Jesus free. The crowd wanted Barabbas set free. Instead of telling them to let Jesus go, Pilate washed his hands, let Barabbas go, and let them have Jesus.

The crowd cried, "Crucify Him!" So the Roman soldiers took Jesus out of the city to the place called Calvary or "Golgotha," which means "the place of the skull." They had made a huge cross to crucify Jesus on.

A great crowd of people followed Jesus and the soldiers. Some were enemies of Jesus, glad to see Him suffer. They did many wicked and painful things to hurt Jesus. Others were friends of Jesus.

Some women followed Him and cried. Jesus turned to them and said, "Do not cry for Me."

The soldiers tried to make Jesus carry His own cross, but soon found He was too weak from His suffering and could not carry it. They chose a man named Simon who was passing by, and they made him carry the cross to its place at Calvary.

When they came to Calvary, the soldiers laid the cross down and stretched Jesus out on it. They drove nails through His hands and feet to fasten Him to the cross. Then they stood the cross upright with Jesus upon it.

While the soldiers were doing this dreadful work, Jesus prayed to God for them. He prayed, "Father, forgive them, for they do not know what they are doing."

Two men who had been robbers and had been sentenced to die were led out to be crucified at the same time with Jesus. One was placed on a cross at His right side and the other at His left. Pilate ordered a sign hung over Jesus' head which read:

"This is Jesus of Nazareth,
The King of the Jews."

The people in the crowd looked at Jesus on the cross and mocked Him. The priests and scribes said, "He saved others, but He cannot save Himself. If You can come down from the cross, we will believe in You!"

Even one of the robbers mocked Jesus, but the second robber scolded him. "Don't you fear God, to talk like that?" he asked. "You are going to die the same way. We deserve to die, but this man has done nothing wrong."

Then this man said to Jesus, "Lord, remember me when You come into Your kingdom!"

Jesus answered him, "Today, you will be with Me in heaven."

Jesus saw His mother Mary and His friend Mary Magdalene standing near the cross. They were filled with sorrow for Him. Also standing nearby was His disciple, John. Jesus asked John to take care of His mother.

Then a sudden darkness came over the land. Jesus cried out, "My God, My God, why have You forsaken Me? It is finished! Father, into Your hands I give My spirit!"

At that moment, there was a loud clap of thunder and the earth shook like an earthquake! The Roman officer, who had charge of the soldiers around the cross, saw what had taken place and how Jesus died. He was afraid and said, "Surely this was the Son of God."

That evening, Joseph of Arimathea, a wealthy man who believed in Jesus, went to Pontius Pilate. He asked Pilate for permission to bury the body of Jesus.

Joseph then took down His body from the cross and wrapped it in fine linen. Nicodemus, another man who believed in Jesus, brought precious spices, which they wrapped up with the body. Then they placed the body in a tomb, which is a cave dug out of a rock. They covered the opening of the tomb with a large stone.

The following morning, some of the people who had helped to crucify Jesus came to Pilate. They reminded him that Jesus had said, "After three days I will rise again." Pilate gave orders that the tomb be watched for three days to make sure that no one tried to take the body away.

Early on the first day of the week, there was a great earthquake. An angel of the Lord came from heaven and rolled back the stone and sat on it. Mary Magdalene and some of the others came to the tomb, found the stone rolled away and saw the angel. The angel told them not to be afraid. Jesus was not there, he said. **He had risen**!

Afterward, Jesus appeared to His disciples and stayed with them for 40 days. Then He was taken up into heaven. Today, when we celebrate Easter, we remember the day that Jesus rose from the dead.